IMAGES
of Wales

SWANSEA
LANDORE, CLYDACH
LLANSAMLET AND MORRISTON

John Davies, farmer of Heol Las Farm, 1909.

IMAGES
of Wales

SWANSEA
LANDORE, CLYDACH
LLANSAMLET AND MORRISTON

Compiled by
André D. Scoville

TEMPUS

First published 2000
Copyright © André D. Scoville, 2000

Tempus Publishing Limited
The Mill, Brimscombe Port,
Stroud, Gloucestershire, GL5 2QG

ISBN 0 7524 2153 0

Typesetting and origination by
Tempus Publishing Limited
Printed in Great Britain by
Midway Clark Printing, Wiltshire

The Castle Gardens development alongside the newly constructed Princess Way that was formerly called Goat Street. After the war the building of 'new' Swansea was quickly planned out and was a credit to the council of the day. It is sad to see such lovely gardens replaced by our modern day 'Castle Square' development.

4

Contents

The author's maternal grandparents Elsie and Dai Gower celebrating their Diamond wedding anniversary in 1980. They were both born in the late 1890s and had resided for the majority of their lives at Morriston. This book is dedicated to them and to André's late aunt, Edna Fraser (née Gower), who while being surrounded with love from her late husband William, her children and grandchildren at Trallwn, fought but lost a courageous fight for life. A final dedication must go to Auntie Megan who has now returned to Morriston but who lived for many years at Cwmbwrla with her late husband Clifford Hughes.

Introduction

Approximately 200 years ago, Swansea was an important seaport as well as being a market town of considerable influence. The old town then lay on the western side of the river Tawe, which was navigable up to the small quay of the first copper works sited at Landore as far back as 1717. At that time, 60-ton boats were arriving here, and at the White Rock copper works of 1720 with their cargoes of copper ore mainly from Cornwall. In the 1811 census, Swansea, including the hamlet of St Thomas had a population of 8,196 with 1,702 houses. The town at this time was about 1½miles long, and its widest point did not exceed ½ a mile. Part of the story of Swansea can be told in reference to its ancient street names, some of them dating back to the twelfth century. They relate to the castle that was the key to the Norman control of the Gower peninsula. The original routes leading to and from the castle's site were earthen tracks. Eventually the tracks nearest the castle were crudely formed into roadways and then built upon. The fourteenth-century street plan remains unchanged even during the second half of the twentieth century in the Strand, High Street, Wind Street, Welcome Lane and Salubrious Passage. As Swansea began to grow, so too did its population when, in 1841 the population of 19,115 rose to 33,972 by 1861; 1881 saw the numbers just top the 50,000 mark which nearly doubled itself by 1901. Two decades later, the population had reached nearly 160,000.

However, sudden change of Swansea's history was to take its toll on the town. It all began at precisely 3.30a.m. on the morning of 27 June 1940. An orange-yellow flare pierced the sky over the sleeping town of Swansea. But before it vanished, a burst of angry bombs bounced and woke up the village of Danygraig. The Luftwaffe had arrived and was to change Swansea forever. Although four of the bombs failed to explode and no one was injured the worst was to come …

It came eight months later: 26 raids, 121 deaths, 285 injuries and more than 5,000 bombs later. It came on the cold, snowy night of 19 February 1941. It was spotted at 7.33p.m. and within minutes Swansea showered bricks and mortar onto roadways and people. Miles of hosepipe inter-wound each other and at almost every moment a water main was shattered, therefore the emergency services were using the docks as a source for water. Most of the town's main services were paralysed and a Mutual Aid Scheme was brought into operation. The shopping centre was a mass of mangled iron, bricks and debris. Evacuation was being conducted at top-speed and as a result of this devastation 7,000 people were homeless; food was short and prayers were being said. For three sleepless nights, the bombs came down and the sirens howled. Exhausted Civil Defence workers tirelessly released trapped victims, fed the hungry and rarely (if at all) thought of their own safety. Forty minutes past midnight on the 22 February, the curtain fell on this 'blitz' that had lasted for a total of 13hrs and 48mins. The population had dropped by 230, including 34 children, and 65 women. Hospital casualty lists had risen by 232. However, through all this Swansea pulled together as everyone was in the same position. On 10 August 1940, an 'Anderson' shelter in Penfilia Road received a direct hit and the five occupants were tragically killed.

Statistics collated at the time of the war are recalled here: 524 times the town came under Warning Siren and in total the raids lasted a total of 1,537 hours. There were 44 raids with 1,494 High Explosive bombs and approximately 35,000 Incendiary bombs dropped on Swansea causing 439 slightly injured people, 412 seriously injured and 387 deaths. Although only 802 premises were destroyed, over 27,000 premises were damaged. The longest Air Raid lasted for 8hrs 56mins and the shortest was 3mins; three Air Raids were without warning. The first Air Raid Warning took place on 1 July 1940 whilst the last Warning closed the chapter on Swansea Town on 14 May 1944.

With the quick action of the County Borough of Swansea, the corporation finally built, with the co-operation of the citizens of Swansea, a town to be proud of. Wide spacious streets renamed Kingsway and Princess Way and a new garden on the former site of the bombed shell of Ben Evans department store. The gardens were a refreshed contrast to the hustle and bustle of shopping. The new Swansea was to be congratulated in 1969 when it was decided that Swansea was to be made a City after receiving HRH Prince Charles as Prince of Wales. Enemy action caused Swansea to be rebuilt but some things remained as strong as the day they were erected. The Mond Buildings, Carlton Cinema, Castle Buildings, Mackworth Hotel and Plaza Cinema to name just a few remained in tact after the war; however Swansea lost the Mackworth and Plaza to bulldozers. Swansea was to gain a new hospital at Singleton but lose the familiar hospital settings of the 'old' but loyal General Hospital. The Dylan Thomas Literature Centre was recently developed at the old Guildhall in Swansea, however, it was only after Thomas' death did Swansea ever acknowledge him. His well-known quotation 'an ugly lovely town' still haunts Swansea to this day.

Even today, Swansea based film, *Twin Town*, used different words to say the same thing, how true it was and is today. The Mumbles Train disappeared only to be replaced by more buses, then supplied by South Wales Transport Company. County Hall was built on the site of the old infirmary; Swansea Leisure Centre on what was the Victoria station and the *South Wales Evening Post* found new premises at Adelaide Street leaving behind memories from Temple Street. Sainsburys supermarket changed the view of Swansea when occupying a well-known site formerly Weavers Flour Mill. High Street, now looking neglected, was at one time one of the busiest streets in the City. However, with the construction of the Quadrant in 1980, businesses transferred to and around this new focal point and then High Street was a ghost street. The last straw came when Woolworth decided to concentrate on their Oxford Street store and this was the final axe to High Street. Recently history has repeated itself in the loss of famous stores: Co-op Living; Dolcis shoe shop; C&A, Menzies and Peters Bookshop. We must inject some life into Swansea or it will die.

A group standing outside the Half Way House public house at Carmel Road, Winch Wen in 1901.

One
Swansea

Oxford Street in 1914, showing the Empire Theatre which was one of the first buildings to be lit with the use of electricity. Opposite is Sidney Palmers' Café which today is the site of Woolworth.

A view over Swansea, c. 1902. The large prominent building is the Swansea 'Free' Library (now called Swansea Central Library) which was opened in 1887 by William Ewart Gladstone. The vacant land adjoining the library was once considered ideal for Studts fair. The church at the bottom right is the Holy Trinity church which was bombed during the blitz of 1941.

A general view over Swansea, c. 1911, after the construction of the Glynn Vivian Art Gallery whose foundation stone was laid by R. Glynn Vivian on 4 May 1909. The Alexandra Skating Rink was later demolished for the building of the Central Police Station in 1913.

Swansea, seen prior to the 'three nights blitz' in February 1941 (above) and after the blitz, c. 1957 (below). Familiar pre-war landmarks have become new roads and roundabouts although you can use Castle Buildings as a guide.

St Mary's church (known at the time as Woodward's church) in 1893. Having been built after the nave of the 'old' church collapsed in 1739, this church was to serve the people of Swansea for approximately 160 years. The need for a larger and more attractive church was planned and, between 1895 and 1897, this church was demolished and rebuilt (as seen below).

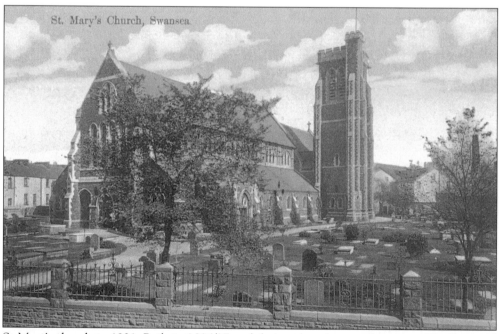

St Mary's church in 1931. Built in 1896/97 and designed to the specifications of Sir Reginald Blomfield, the church served Swansea well until three nights in February 1941. Note the houses on the left now the site of Littlewoods.

The shell of St Mary's church after the three nights blitz. It remained like this for many years until renovation work commenced.

St Mary's parish church completed and photographed in 1962. The re-consecration by Bishop, and former vicar Jack Thomas took place on the 28 May 1959 in the presence of Queen Elizabeth, The Queen Mother.

13

This rare photograph taken at an unusual height in 1901 shows Wind Street with the statue of Sir Henry Hussey Vivian (1821-1894) which was erected here in March 1896 on the site of the former Island House. The statue stood here until December 1936 when it was removed due to traffic problems and resurrected at Victoria Park. The statue was again removed in 1981 and placed in the newly constructed St David's Square, near St Mary's church. The large building on the left was Ben Evans department store (no relation to David Evans).

Ben Evans department store, photographed here around 1910, opened in 1894 and was built on the site of the fourteenth-century Plas House. This enormous store acquired entrances from Castle Street, Caer Street and Goat Street (now Princess Way). One of the worst casualties of the three nights blitz on the town in February 1941, the store was reduced to just a shell. The site was later transformed into the pleasant Castle Gardens.

The devastation after the horrific bombing to Swansea over the 21/22/23 February, 1941. A huge amount of the town of Swansea was wiped out. As can be seen, not many buildings survived.

When Swansea was rebuilt after the war, one of its most endearing features was Castle Gardens, built on the site of Ben Evans Department Store which had been sadly gutted by fire after the three nights blitz. In later years the trees and bushes were allowed to grow large causing the gardens to appear very isolated. However, as this photograph shows, the gardens provided a pleasant break from the hustle and bustle of shopping and were only recently altered into Castle Square – concreted for the occasional concert, making a canvas for chalk drawings and skate-boarders! If the trees and bushes from the gardens were kept low, general opinion is that Castle Gardens could have been a beautiful attraction to the centre of Swansea. Boots the chemist pictured here remained at this site until the Quadrant Centre opened in 1980. Today the building is McDonalds restaurant. The photograph was taken in 1968.

The Theatre Royal on the corner of Temple Street and Goat Street (now Princess Way) in 1894. The theatre was built in 1806 and opened a year later. The 'Tudor Gothic' tower in the background belonged to the post office which later became the home of the *South Wales Daily Post*.

The same view in 1910. After the demolition of the Theatre Royal in 1897, David Evans department store was built and opened in 1900. The building was a very fine example of architecture, the façade being of ornamental bath stone. Opposite David Evans are Temple Buildings which replaced the police station around 1874. Today it is the site of Castle Square development.

On the night of the 21 February 1941, David Evans department store, in common with so many others, was completely destroyed in the Air Raid. Fortunately the members of the staff on fire duty were able, with some difficulty, to make their escape from the building and there was no loss of life.

Gradually over the years following 1941, the David Evans store were able to re-establish itself, and to concentrate almost all the business activities and departments in the High Street Arcade area, leaving only the china and hardware departments some distance away, in Oxford Street. Before the Arcade, in High Street could be used, it had to be completely re-roofed. The site of the old store in Goat Street remained an open space, but as time went on, difficulties over reconstruction and restrictions of materials and labour continually arose. At last news came that David Evans could be rebuilt almost on the exact site. The grand re-opening of David Evans department store (seen here in 1999), took place at their new Princess Way premises on 29 October, 1954.

Oxford Street in 1906 with Boots Cash Chemist alongside Myrddin Davies Cash Chemist. The site was occupied for many years by the Co-op Living department store.

Looking at the destruction from Temple Street towards Oxford Street as a result of Luftwaffe bombers in February 1941. The frontage of the market remained standing; however, the market's interior remained a smouldering wreck. It was quickly cleared of rubble and opened as an outdoor market lasting for many years.

Oxford Street with cars whizzing past via Princess Way in 1978. Richard shops have recently closed along with Living (then just called Co-op) and Dolcis shoe shop. One important difference is that this part of Oxford Street was open to traffic.

Oxford Street in 1990, showing the Living Store and BHS (British Home Stores) and Marks & Spencer.

Oxford Street in 1912 showing the Waterloo Hotel on the left and the old façade of the second Oxford Street Market which was built in 1897 having been constructed on the site of the original Oxford Street Market of 1830. The building in this photograph was built with red Ruabon bricks with bath stone dressings.

Oxford Street towards the junction of Waterloo Street, around 1934. Familiar shops before the war, however, things were to change…

Looking down Oxford Street towards the junction of Waterloo Street, north and south, c. 1944. Today the land on the left is occupied by Topshop and Next, Marks & Spencer now occupy the land on the right.

OXFORD STREET, SWANSEA   W 8171

The rebirth of Oxford Street photographed in 1962 shows Wymans on the left which became Menzies. Incidentally, Waterloo Street now only exists on the corner of Wymans; the site at one time occupied by the Waterloo Hotel. The shops and entrance to the third Swansea Market were completely rebuilt and officially opened on 18 May 1961.

College Street, *c.* 1936. The white centre building occupied by Dunn & Co. men's outfitters was demolished to widen Welcome Lane leading to the Strand. College Street has recently been opened again for traffic after being pedestrianized.

High Street in 1913 with the newly built Hotel Cameron on right. The original Cameron Arms Hotel was demolished in 1910 for this grand building.

211808.

This 1934 photograph depicts a slightly different scene with the Hotel Cameron ceasing to trade a couple of years earlier, and F.W. Woolworth and cafeteria then occupied the premises. This beautiful building was bombed, in 1941, during the Second World War and then rebuilt.

Woolworths in June 1986 just days before it closed its doors for the last time. Argos now occupies the majority of the building as Woolworth remain the owners.

Holy Trinity church on Alexandra Road, bombed during the blitz in 1941, but demolished in 1956. Today, flats occupy the site and are named Trinity Court. Near to this site remains The Ragged School, founded in 1847 and rebuilt in 1911. The foundation stones were laid by Roger Beck and Miss E. A. Dillwyn on 24 August 1911. Today the building is used for the Centre For Spiritual Awareness.

Wind Street looking towards the bridge in 1904.

Mount Street towards Wind Street, *c.* 1903. At the time of this photograph this area was the heart of a port and dockland area as some of the offices were contained here. The building on the left is the Sailors' Home in Victoria Road which had connections with the Sailors' Mission Chapel in Adelaide Street. The home was demolished in the 1960s along with the iron bridge.

Swansea Board of Guardians 1895. It was these people who administered and ruled the Workhouse at Mount Pleasant.

Men of Dawnays constructional engineers works in 1920. Situated at King's Dock Works, they specialized in the design, fabrication and erection of riveted and welded steel framed structures of every description.

Swansea Sands in 1903.

Queuing patiently to reach the beach at The Slip in 1919. On the left is the signal box for the Victoria Line. The queue at the front are waiting to purchase railway tickets from the shed on the right.

Another view of Swansea Sands from the Slip on a less busy day. Swansea beaches, including this one at the Slip, were considered to be the best in Britain and so the sand was transported to northern resorts.

As a result, this similar view from the late 1970s shows a very different beach. In the background is the new County Hall but the Victoria Line and the people have all disappeared!

The Guildhall looking towards St Helen's Road. Part of the Guildhall viewed in this photograph is the Brangwyn Hall named after Frank Brangwyn who painted the famous panels that hang in the hall today. Painted for the Houses of Commons when he eventually finished them it was discovered that they were too large. We are indeed very fortunate to hold them in Swansea.

Main Entrance to Council Chamber, Guildhall, Swansea.

The Guildhall in 1944. The building was officially opened on 23 October 1934. Constructed on what was part of Victoria Park (then a site of more than 2 acres), the foundation stone was laid by Alderman David Williams MP, and David Matthews on 4 May 1932.

South Dock in 1907.

South Dock in 1963 is now recognizable as what became Swansea Marina. On the left is the site that was to become luxury flats while the Pump House is today a restaurant.

Ma and I here – July 30. 1904.

Mumbles village in 1904. Today the scene is quite different with the construction of Knab Rock in the 1980s and Mumbles lifeboat launched in 1905 and lighthouse.

W 1091   THE PIER, MUMBLES.

Mumbles Pier.

'It should never have ended'. This is what everybody says when any mention is made of the oldest passenger railway in the world. Pictured here in the late 1950s, the Mumbles Railway was established by an Act of Parliament of 1804 and began operating in 1806, the first passenger traffic starting the following year. Originally horse-drawn, the service became steam train between 1878 and 1929. March 1929 saw electrification of the line when tramcars such as this were used. The Mumbles Railway closed on 5 January 1960.

Limeslade Bay in the mid-1960s.

Caswell Bay, photographed, c. 1925, was considered one of the most popular bays in the Swansea area. In the distance on the right is the windmill built in 1881 in connection with Oystermouth Waterworks. By the 1850s the supplies of drinking water in the Oystermouth area had become quite inadequate especially considering the increase in population. As a result, in 1879, the Oystermouth Waterworks Company was set up, obtaining water from springs at the western side of Caswell Bay and pumping it to Kiln Green service reservoir at Newton. Although this took place throughout 1882 it was not a great success.

Elba Crescent, St Thomas holding a street party to celebrate the Coronation of Queen Elizabeth II on 2 June 1953.

A class photograph from Gwyrosydd Infants' School in 1975. Left to right, back row: -?- (class teacher), Andrew Smith, Andrew Watts, Andrew Grigg, Ian Colfer, Robert Britton, Gareth Owen, Stephen Hurford, Andrew Jones, Ian Wilkinson, Simon Morgan, Paul Killa, Mrs Evans (headmistress). Front row: Paul Rix, Nicola Turner, Cheryl O'Connor, Beverley Jenkins, Louise Pavlou, Michelle Lewis, Lisa Myers, Joanne Austin, Karen Stevens, Suzanne Sylvie, Alison Campbell, Paul Wheel.

Manselton in 1908. This area was part of the medieval manor of Millwood and later formed part of the Mansel Estate; it consisted mainly of farmland until the 1880s. Numerous coalmines occupied this area from an early date, the main ones being Mansel Colliery, Pwll-y-Domen and Graig Colliery. When coal became established, the Mansel family began to develop a residential area on a planned grid layout similar to earlier designs for Morriston streets. The early street names which still exist today were named after members of the Mansel family – Courtenay Street, Cecil Street and Robert Street.

Dyfatty Infants' School in 1974. A clean-up programme set up in the Greenhill area was followed by the building of multi-storey flats and Dyfatty Infants' School to educate the large numbers of children. It eventually became a school for the physically handicapped which moved from Morfydd House School.

Parklands Primary School class of 1977/78. The headmistress, Mrs Thomas standing on the left, is joined by class teacher Miss Rees on the right.

A sad farewell to a shop that has been in Swansea for more than fifty years. C&A announced nationally that they are to close all their British shops at the end of 2000. This photograph was taken from where HSBC (Midland Bank) stands today in Portland Street. This building is occupied by Mothercare today. The store moved in 1980 to the newly created Quadrant where it remained until closure this year. Two brothers, Clemens and August (C&A) left their home in Mettingen, Germany and opened a warehouse in Sneek, Holland in 1841. C&A opened in Great Britain in 1922.

The Kingsway only partly rebuilt after the Second World War. Dated 1955 it shows the C&A store (now Mothercare) and the Burlington restaurant and café, now the site of Halifax Building Society. On the right (as in the previous photograph) is the single storey post office building. In the background is the side of the Plaza Cinema.

St Helen's Road and Picton Place, c. 1922. Swansea and South Wales Institution for the Blind were housed in the buildings on the left prior to moving to Morriston in 1930. The premises photographed here were demolished and replaced with the Plaza Cinema. Today this road is known as the Kingsway with a nightclub and the vacant Tesco store occupying the site.

The Plaza Cinema, 1931-1965. Swansea's finest cinema in Swansea, situated on the Kingsway, was replaced by the Odeon Cinema Group in 1967 with a large Tesco store occupying the ground floor.

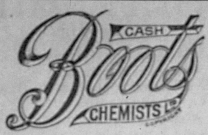

High Street in 1870 with the first Great Western railway station which opened in 1850. Opposite is Boots Cash Chemist (see advertisement on the opposite page).

The same view eighty years later in 1950. The GWR station is now called Swansea station but had undergone two transformations, one in 1924-26 when the eastern platform was added and another in 1934-35 when a new façade was added. Boots the Chemist remains unaltered.

High Street's most famous store Lewis Lewis in 1972 prior to closure. Situated on the corner of High Street and King's Lane it was established on this site for more than 140 years. Today, Iceland occupies the site.

Mackworth Hotel, High Street, in 1910. Four shops up from Lewis Lewis, this hotel was built in 1899 and was the second hotel with the name. The original Mackworth Hotel in Wind Street had been demolished to make way for the new post office. This Mackworth was itself demolished in 1968 after surviving the devastating blitz on the town. Today it is the site of Alexandra House.

Alexandra church taken in 1972 prior to demolition. It was situated at Alexandra Road now the site of the Oldway Centre.

A photograph of the construction of the Oldway Centre and Alexandra House in 1974, prior to completion in 1975. Also in the photograph is the back of the now demolished Elim church. It moved up the road and is now called The City Temple.

Hopkin Morgan Bakery and Madame Foner, Corsetieres, situated at High Street in 1962.

On the opposite side of the road, in 1962, was Littlewoods, Halfords and Home & Colonial. Note the traffic warden on the left of the photograph and the fact that there are no bus lanes, bus stops or any cars.

St Helen's Road in 1910. On the left today is Brunswick Health Centre and HomeGower House residential home. Opposite are houses with their original frontage. Out of the photograph on the right is the Brunswick Methodist church. In the background are the distinctive towers of St Andrew's Scottish church now closed and vandalized.

Staff of Manor Bakery situated at St Helen's Road, c. 1960. Manor Bakery was owned by D. Ayres Jones and specializing in 'Mono' equipment for bakeries. His shops in Cwmbwrla, Manselton and St Helen's Road were extremely popular for high-class confectionery. Pictured left to right: Eunice Early, Joan Gower, Pamela Hann, Mrs Thomas.

SWANSEA HOSPITAL.

Swansea General Hospital at St Helen's Road in 1904. The hospital had been visited by the eminent Florence Nightingale; it was officially opened on Wednesday 27 October 1869 at a cost of £14,000. Only the clock tower (pictured here) and an annex building on Philips Parade exist today. The remainder of the hospital has been demolition and rebuilt as a residential home named HomeGower House.

Members of the Voluntary Aid Detachment of the British Red Cross in Swansea pose for a photograph in 1930. They include: Mrs Hawken, Mrs Ellen Harvey, Mrs Edward Morgan, Mrs Macdonald, Miss Knill, Mrs Gammon, Miss W. Nice, Miss M. Moy Evans, Miss Ronnie Jones. The work of the VAD was extended to the Territorial Army in a field day on Bishopston Common. They helped the District Nurses, assisted with the housekeeping at Swansea Hospital during holiday periods, and actually staffed a ward for a fortnight. The most comprehensive first-aid service offered by the Division was to the Boy Scout camp at Margam in 1928, when responsibility was undertaken for the care of 3,000 scouts, including Baden Powell himself, who remarked, 'The Red Cross is here. Excellent!' During the week, 230 cases were dealt with most efficiently. Most of them were wasp stings, burns and sprains; but there were 30 bed cases, 3 of which were sent on to Bridgend hospital for surgery.

The Family Practitioner Committee department of the NHS in 1987. David John (front left), administrator, is seen presenting a retirement present to Thomas Evans (front right) surrounded by the staff.

Chairman of the Family Practitioner Committee, Dr Paul Mellor, is photographed in June 1990 presenting a retirement present to Registrar, Annice Lewis.

The Staff of Contractor Services within Iechyd Morgannwg Health in March 1999. They were photographed at the retirement of Director, George Plunkett, who is seated in the centre.

A view from the entrance of St Mary's church in 1973. On the right is Swansea Market and in the background is Thomas Thomas & Sons Ltd, wholesalers, today the premises is occupied by Abbey National. On this site since 1980 is the Quadrant shopping centre with the entrance to the now departing C&A store.

Laying the finishing touches to the newly built Quadrant shopping centre, built on what was Orange Street and Wassail Square. This part is used as a bus terminus.

Swansea in 1980. The British Telecom tower can be seen next to Swansea Castle creating a vast contrast between old and new. More changes have occurred, even since 1980: Castle Gardens has since been concreted, the shop on the right has been demolished and the BT tower has been revamped.

Two
Hafod, Landore and Plasmarl

In approximately 1730, the Swansea district of Hafod (translated means 'summer dwelling') was a vastly different place than today. Along with Cwmbwrla and Kilvey, Hafod was a noted place of beauty. The landscape dotted by a few farms, and a mansion placed in the hills commanded a view of rolling meadows, rich with stately oak trees. However, the introduction of copper ore smelting and other industries to Swansea and in particular Hafod, meant economic prosperity and expansion for the town but as usual the natural scenery paid a heavy price. The Hafod ferry (pictured here) commenced in the early 1800s and continued to carry passengers along the River Tawe until February 1945.

Hafod Canal in 1923. This photograph shows the last barge and ostler with his horse. The Vivians' barges were always made available to children for their Sunday and Bank Holiday outings to Clydach and further up the valley. Incredibly, in mid-Victorian times, not only horses but men and women used to pull the canal barges laden with coal from Morriston and Landore to the various works. Occasionally, if the load was very heavy, small steamboats were used along the route.

Hafod Canal in 1961. Today some of these buildings stand in ruins near the Landore roundabout. Two chimney stacks remain to this day as the whole site has been left to decay. The canal was filled in mid-1960s.

Hafod blast furnaces highlighting the prosperity in this part of Swansea in the 1950s.

A view of Hafod Park and St John's parish church in 1971. The photograph was taken from the Hafod tip now the site of Pentrehafod Comprehensive School.

A view of the Hafod Copper Works, in 1810, which were constructed by Messrs Vivian & Son. The Hafod Works played an immense part in the industrial growth of nineteenth-century Swansea.

A sketch of the same Hafod Copper Works in 1850. Note how many houses now surround the chimneys. For 114 years the Hafod Works was linked with the interests and fortunes of the Vivian family: from Vivian & Sons in 1810; to Vivian & Sons Ltd in 1916; British Copper Manufacturers (merger) in 1924; ICI (amalgamation) in 1928; Yorkshire Imperial Metals (merger) in 1957; until it was finally abandoned in the 1980s.

Vivian & Sons Ltd No.1 Shed with Garratt locomotive in the 1920s.

The last two remaining chimney stacks in Swansea. This area should be preserved, as it is a final trace of Swansea's industrial history. The V&S No. 1 Shed remains partly derelict alongside a landscaped cycle path.

An aerial photograph of Hafod in the 1970s.

Graig Trewyddfa, Landore in 1885. If you imagine this view without roads and buildings you will have an idea of how beautiful this part of Swansea was in 1700. Cwm Pit (in the centre left) was situated at the bottom of Trewyddfa Road. It was established around 1720 and was worked out and closed in about 1902. St Peter's Roman Catholic church now occupies the site. Today the main road at the bottom of the mountain is Cwm Level Road (known locally as the 'Black Road' for obvious reasons) leading to Brynhyfred.

Landore Cinema on Neath Road in the 1970s. 'The Bug' Cinema, as it was affectionately called, was situated on Neath Road. Today a privately owned company occupies the building.

Neath Road, Landore, in January 1981. On the corner of Field Street and Neath Road was Swansea Aerials and Video Film Hire (this being of note as the video recorder had only recently been invented).

The same view in April 2000. Neath Road now intersects with the large Landore roundabout whose nearby bypass has reduced traffic on this old road. Notice Morris Castle high on the left which was built to house workers of Robert Morris's Landore and Plasmarl collieries around 1750.

Neath Road, as seen here in 1981, is completely different today. The houses on the immediate left were demolished and the site is now the car park of the popular Pizzeria Vesuvio Restaurant at 200 Neath Road.

The Red Lion Inn and Police Box in 1981 near the turning for Station Road. Both were synonymous with Landore and have both disappeared.

The Siemens Laboratory landmark that adjoined wasteland (once the canal and railway) and Neath Road prior to demolition in the early 1980s. The Landore-Siemens Steelworks had an eventful history. When it started it was described as covering almost 100 acres of land on both sides of the Tawe and was conveniently sited to have excellent communication with the Great Western and Swansea Vale Railways.

Landore wasteland and slurry. The slag tips are man-made mountains removed when Swansea City Council cleaned up the area after works were left abandoned.

The Llandore Viaduct near Swansea.

The original Landore viaduct in 1850 designed by the world famous engineer of the Great Western Railway, Isambard Kingdom Brunel. Work on the Landore viaduct began on 2 August 1847 and the South Wales Railway down to Swansea was opened using the viaduct on the 18 June 1850.

A view of the 'new' viaduct (taken around 1950) which opened for service in October 1889. The houses on the left are today Rossi's Fish & Chip shop. The Act for the Swansea Canal was passed in 1794 and the Canal above (also depicted in the top photograph) was completed in 1798. Here the canal is alongside the railway which is today the Landore Bypass.

Two views of the Swansea Canal at Landore in 1943.

Another 1850 view of Brunel's viaduct from Plasmarl looking towards Landore.

The Morfa Stadium at Landore in its infancy. This photograph dated from August 1986 and shows the reclamation of land which had once been heavy laden with industry now used for recreational purposes. The Swansea Athletics Track (its original name) was opened by the Mayor Councillor Alan Lloyd on the 5 October, 1980.

Plasmarl roundabout in 1980. The photographs shows the prominent remains of the railway along with landmarks of today such as St Paul's church situated on the corner of the 'Black Road' and Neath Road.

Stewart & Lloyd Dinner held at High Street's Mackworth Hotel, Swansea, in the mid-1950s.

An early school photograph of Plasmarl Council Boys, Standard 7, in 1913.

Plasmarl Girls School, Standard 4, in 1920.

Plasmarl Elementary Boys in 1943.

Locals stand outside the Red Cow Inn situated at Neath Road, Plasmarl prior to an outing in 1918.

Three
Llangyfelach
and Penllergaer

Llangyfelach Square in 1900.

Bishop Cyfelach of Glamorgan is believed to have been the founder of the Christian Church here at Llangyfelach in the eighth century although the church seen here is a replacement of the original building. The church records date from 1690 and are written in Latin. The churchyard in Llangyfelach covers an area of nearly four acres; it was the central burial ground for an extremely large parish of 27,693 acres closing for new burials in 1893 and only allowing burials to take place in family graves where there was space. There are only three towers detached from their churches in Wales and one is at Llangyfelach. By the end of the eighteenth century, the church had been allowed to fall into disrepair and as a result of a heavy gale, during the Napoleonic wars, the eastern side of the belfry collapsed onto the original church and it consequently had to be demolished.

On the east side of the tower there is an arch that would have been the entrance into the former church. The first vicars of Llangyfelach church were Aggerw and Clydno in 1066.

An ancient stone at Llangyfelach church, dating from the tenth century.

Plough and Harrow village football team at Llangyfelach in 1900.

The Plough and Harrow public house alongside Llangyfelach church in September 1986.

Bethel chapel at Llangyfelach at the turn of the twentieth century. The photograph was taken prior to alterations to the chapel.

Bethel chapel in September 1986.

Penllergaer House, *c.* 1905. The Prices, in about 1710, build a tall three-storey, five-bay residence that passed to John Llewelyn of Ynysgerwn. In 1800 he built an adjoining two-storey block with 'canted bows' on the side, in a style that suggests William Jernegan. Malkin in 1803 described it as 'a new house in good style, not far removed from magnificence'. Then in 1835-36 Edward Haycock demolished the Price house and enlarged and altered the rest with a two-storey portico with an elliptical staircase hall and a circular room. These alterations were made for the notable scientist and botanist John Dillwyn Llewelyn who filled the gardens and an orchid house with rare and beautiful plants. However, after the death of Sir John Llewelyn MP, in 1927, there followed a decline in the fabric of the building and it was occupied temporarily for institutional use only. The house was blown up in 1961. The council offices of Lliw Valley Borough Council were later built on the site.

In its day the Penllergaer estate was an outstanding example of a picturesque landscape created by John Dillwyn Llewellyn. Born in 1810, he was distinguished for not only his designs to the landscape but also for his photographic experiments; he died in 1882. Today part of the Penllergaer estate is now part of the motorway and service station. These photographs show the building and opening of the Melin Llan bridge at Penllergaer, c. 1912.

Penllergaer Council School, *c.* 1925.

Four

Clydach

Station and Glanyravon Works, Clydach.

The village of Clydach is very much industrialized, with the most important nickel works in the world. The village grew out of the ancient district of Rhyndwyglydach in the parish of Llangyfelach. In 1847 Rhyndwyglwdach was made into an independent parish and adjustments were made to bring the new parish into line with the realities of the village people. The oldest part of the village, Aberclydach, was included in the parish. In 1901, when the population of the parish reached a total of 4,462, Clydach saw the founding of the Mond Nickel Works, Clydach railway station, and Glanyrafon works (now Clydach Market) was used by Rees & Kirby. This postcard dates from 1928.

The Square, Clydach, in 1910. A very large crowd gathered here in 1907 on the occasion of the unveiling of the Horse Trough in front of the Public Hall (pictured on the left) in memory of Temperance worker W. H. Lewis. It is now sited in Forge Fach Parc. Note the Cook's Arms on the right.

The Cook's Arms which was demolished for road widening in 1968. The landlord and his son stand on the left.

High Street and the hospital, *c*. 1950.

Two Clydach shops, *c*. 1916.

The New Church, Clydach-on-Tawe

St Mary's church, Clydach, in 1910.

High Street looking towards Clydach's St Mary's church in 1936.

High Street in 1930 when the horse and carriage era was being taken over by cars.

The Mond Works in 1949. Ludwig Mond came to Clydach in 1901 to set up an industrial plant because there was rail access to the port of Swansea and to anthracite coal from Terenni Gleision, a few miles up the Swansea valley.

The Mond Works painters, *c.* 1920.

Two splendid photographs of the Mond Nickel Works Bicycle Club in 1910 standing outside the offices and inside the Works.

An early twentieth century photograph of E. Lloyd, a Brook Street baker of Clydach.

Mrs A Bolton, Commandant of the Clydach Detachment of the Red Cross instructing Cadets in 'Mothercraft', c. 1960.

Five
Llansamlet

The village of Llansamlet grew up around Llansamlet Square. This photograph, dating back to 1900, shows the original Star Inn and the Smiths Arms.

Church Road showing the first Llansamlet church tower in 1900. This road was the centre of the original village before the turnpike road was built in the late 1700s. Opposite the church is the old church hall. Canal Man's Cottage situated on the left is now the site of the Plough & Harrow public house.

The same view as above in 1982. The Plough & Harrow was on the left and opposite was the Llansamlet Sunday schoolroom.

The interior of the previous Llansamlet church. St Samlet's church at Llansamlet is the mother church of the manor of Kilvey. Its position was selected especially for the rising ground above the marsh. The first church was built around 1720 and was described in 1878 as being a 'small and dilapidated structure of no historic interest and unsightly'.

Interior of the present Llansamlet church in 1986. Foundations for this building were begun in 1876 on land given by the Earl of Jersey. The foundation stone laid in 1878 by his wife, the Countess of Jersey. An Early English design was used by architect, Mr Clark, who used local labour to build the church at a cost of £6,500, although, because of a shortage of money the tower was not added until 1915. This church holds a capacity of 645 people.

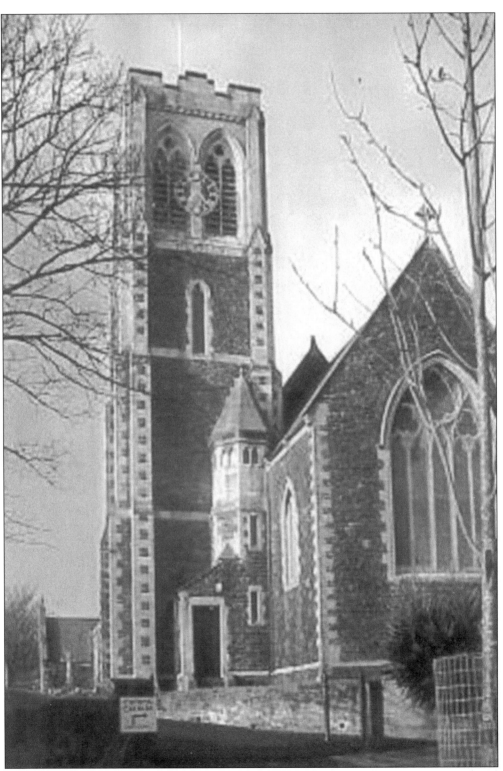

Llansamlet church today.

Llansamlet Fair in 1906. Note the 'new' church with 'old' tower.

Children playing on land near the graveyard of Llansamlet church in 1943. In the 1700s the Church Pit was the most important in the area as it drained many of the other collieries via its large fire engine or steam pump. It was 80ft deep. New shafts were sunk in 1824 when the workings were extended. It was later renamed Charles Pit after the owner, Charles Henry Smith.

The men and boys of Samlet Colliery in 1898. The pit was 100yds deep and was sunk in the late eighteenth century as Gwen Pit. It was finally closed in 1930. It was situated near Gwernllwynchwith Road.

Llansamlet Flute Band in 1915.

GWR railway station at Llansamlet, *c*. 1922. On the top of the embankment on the left (out of sight) were Mattie's Cottages.

Mattie's Cottages (now demolished) in the early 1950s. They were situated in front of Llwyncrwn Road.

The brave ARP (Air Raid Precaution) Wardens at Brynawel, Frederick Place, in 1940. Four messengers are sitting at the front. One such messenger, Reginald Galvin who lived at 12 Brynawel, Llansamlet, was killed in Neath Road, Landore, on 10 August 1941. His name appears in the County Borough of Swansea Roll of Honour for members of the Civil Defence Services who were killed by Enemy Action.

This is a rare photograph of bombed houses at Frederick Place – the photographer was breaking the law to record the devastation that wrecked homes and lives during the Second World War. Although it is often recalled that Swansea town centre bombed heavily, and almost wiped out, the villages were also often hit as a result of German bombs. On 22 April 1941, two parachute mines landed at Frederick Place, one exploded wrecking houses and damaging many others and consequently thirteen people were injured.

The biggest works to dominate Llansamlet from 1876 to 1974 were those belonging to the Swansea Imperial Smelting Corporation Ltd, called Swansea Vale Works and seen here in 1957. Originally called the Swansea Vale Spelter Company Ltd, the works was formed in 1876; John Griffiths was appointed chairman of the company and Richard Martin its secretary and managing director. Between 1920 and 1930, the market became so critical that all the zinc smelters in the area (apart from Swansea Vale) closed down permanently.

By the 1960s, the Swansea Vale Works (part of the Rio Tinto Zinc Corporation – RTZ) was providing employment for over 800 jobs. However, as this photograph shows, the destruction and pollution had taken its toll on the Swansea Valley. When boardroom directors from RTZ reviewed the situation they found that their Avonmouth plant was a cleaner and refreshed way of producing zinc and so the announcement was made that, after nearly 100 years, the Swansea Vale Works was to close on 21 June 1974.

The Nantyffin gates of Swansea Vale Works in the early 1970s. A report from the RTZ Company included estimates that some tips on the site of the Swansea Vale Works contained between 11 to 30 per cent lead, in addition to high zinc levels. Around 700 tons of the richest of these tip materials were subsequently taken by road to Avonmouth for further metal extraction. Having acquired the site of the Swansea Vale Works, Swansea City Council continued to operate the treatment works on the site for a further two and a half years. The cost of maintaining this plant was £66,952. It was part of the original plan to keep the newly constructed three-storey office block and incorporate it into the new site development, but a detailed investigation of the structure revealed the presence of high alumina cement which had produced serious deterioration of the reinforced concrete frame. The whole site was subsequently demolished and landscaped.

The Swansea Enterprise Zone Information Centre situated on Samlet Road in 1981. Swansea City Council bought the land to all the heavy industrial sites and, as a result, took on the massive task of regenerating the land for development. One of the largest retail companies to open on the newly developed enterprise zone was Ukay & Dodge City, furniture and DIY store (later becoming B&Q). The first roads were established causing much confusion but eventually the Swansea Enterprise Park settled down to become a necessary part of Swansea. This building is today the site of Samlet Social Club & Hyper Value.

A class photograph from Llansamlet Junior Comprehensive School in 1984, all aged around twelve years old. Left to right, back row: André Scoville, Christopher Hazelwood, Darren Hamer, Fraser Morris, Mark Russell, Steven Newman, Robert Buchan. Second row from the back: Jason Thrupp, Richard Fenwick, Emma Jones, Joanne Jones, Suzanne Watts, Donna Smith, Simon John, Andrew Payne. Third row: Cathy Rogers, Caroline Haste, Donna Marie Ross, Mrs Cynthia Davies (form tutor), Sara Harkness, Beverley Hopkins, Emma Wright. Front row: Richard Harris, Mark Williams.

The village of Lonlas, *c.* 1929. The photograph is taken looking towards Main Road while on the left is the Bowens Arms. Some buildings in this photograph were either altered or demolished as a result of the construction of the M4 motorway.

Lonlas in the mid-1960s after the construction of the roundabout. The Bowen's Arms is out of the photograph on the right but on the left is the site that was to open on 28 August 1972 as the M4 from Lonlas to Llangyfelach. This was built to reduce traffic density on the A48 road passing through Llansamlet.

Six
Birchgrove and Glais

Birchgrove Colliery, c. 1890. The collieries of Llansamlet and Birchgrove feature conspicuously in the story of eighteenth-century mining activities locally. Chauncey Townsend opened up the first collieries here in about 1750, on land leased to him by the Morgan family. Townsend was an important and influential citizen of London, being an alderman of the city. His daughter married John Smith who later opened mines in this area. He was succeeded, in 1797, after his death by his two sons, Charles and Henry. After the construction of the Swansea Canal was completed in 1798, a tramway was laid which ran in the direction of Cwmbwrla. Charles Smith then erected an iron rail tramway to replace a more primitive one built earlier by Townsend which was used to speed up deliveries of coal from Birchgrove through Foxhole to the port. The Birchgrove Colliery was opened around 1830 and closed 1928.

Birchgrove Colliery in 1919. Although a housing estate occupies the site of the colliery today, the office building in the photograph is still standing today at Birchgrove Road.

The miners' rescue team of Birchgrove Colliery in 1923.

Smith's Row, Birchgrove, in 1903. On the left is old Nazareth chapel (1862-1906).

Birchgrove Road in 1930. On the immediate left is the Terrace Inn. The photograph shows both Nazareth chapels. The 'new' chapel in the centre of the photograph was sadly demolished in 1996.

Birchgrove Council School showing the old school building and yard in 1915. The new Birchgrove School opened on the same site in 1990. It is now attended by 900 children aged between 11 and 16 years from the villages of Birchgrove, Glais and Clydach together with children from other areas.

Standard I in 1915. The headmaster is Mr. E. H. Thomas.

Standard VI and VII in 1915.

The teachers of Birchgrove School in 1915. Left to right, back row: Irene Thomas, Maggie Aldridge, Glyn R. Thomas, Maria Power. Front row: Gwen Hannah Rosser, E. H. Thomas (headmaster); Miss Donne, Miss Sims.

Birchgrove Rugby Club 1927/28. The captain is Selwyn Morris (holding the ball).

Birchgrove RFC in the 1939/40 season.

A wedding photograph taken of a Birchgrove family in 1898. The men at the back, left to right are: David Watkins, David Morris (brother of bride), William Morris (father of bride). Front row: Mary Watkins, Jenkin Davies (bridegroom), Martha Morris (bride), William Donne (grandfather of bride). All four young men were miners at Birchgrove Colliery.

Deacons from Nazareth Welsh Calvinistic Methodist chapel at Birchgrove in 1902. Left to right, back row, standing: Thomas Rowland, Edward H. Thomas, David J. Thomas. Front row, seated: John Ley, James Maddock, Philip Jones, Daniel Thomas, William Clement.

Nazareth Chapel Ladies Guild, *c.* 1960.

A street party at Old Road, Birchgrove, held for the Coronation of King George VI in May 1937.

Festival of Britain celebrations taking place outside Benny Edwards' Garage at Birchgrove in 1951.

The local Calvinistic Methodist monthly meeting, which was held at Nazareth Chapel, Birchgrove, seen here in 1911. The lady with the large hat in centre is advertising her family's millinery business.

Glais Road, Birchgrove. This road is now part of and called Birchgrove Road. On the left is Benny Edwards' Garage.

Glais School in 1901.

Members of the Sunday School class of St Paul's church, Glais, in 1898.

The old Glais bridge which was built in 1806 and demolished in 1990. A new stone bridge was built on its site.

Seven

Morriston

Morriston Star Laundry, a popular image in the minds of Morriston inhabitants. The drivers are photographed here alongside a van bearing the locally familiar name. Founded by the Gardiner family of Springfield Street, the business grew and prospered at Bush Road before closing around 1969/70. Near to its site today is McDonalds restaurant and Matalan.

Mary Gower (left) sitting on the steps of Tycoch Cottages, under the supervision of neighbour Mrs Thomas. Tycoch was demolished in 1938 after more than 256 years of nonconformist worship had taken place in these thatched cottages.

Morriston Scouts led by a much loved and respected man, the late, Iorwerth Lewis. He was well-known for his appearances as Father Christmas at Woodfield Street and Morriston isn't the same without him.

In June 1921, a company of Girl Guides and Brownies were formed. The first Officers were: Margaret Jones (captain), Doris Williams (lieutenant), and Muriel Hanney (lieutenant) who was also Brown Owl. This photograph was taken in the Parish Hall in 1940.

Prime Minister David Lloyd George addressing Morriston at Morriston Cross outside the shop that was once Alan Hole newsagents on Clase Road in 1918. Pompa's Cross Café and Craven Hairdresser & Tobacconist are next door.

The old Lamb and Flag Hotel at Morriston Cross surrounded by soldiers listening to the Prime Minister on his tour around Wales.

Pentrepoeth Girls School, Standard 2B, in 1920.

Staff of Hopkin Morgan taken in the offices at Lower Morfydd Street (now Room at the Top) in 1952.

A rare photographs of the Morriston Orpheus Choir and Ivor Sims on stage with Sir Harry Secombe in November 1957. They were called upon to attend a Royal Command Performance at the London Palladium. The Orpheus were to appear a year earlier but it was cancelled when the Queen thought it inappropriate to attend at the same time as the Suez Crisis. The Morriston Orpheus also appeared with Tommy Trinder on ATV's top Sunday night show, *Sunday Night at the London Palladium*. The conductor was Ivor Sims, the deputy conductor was Elwyn A. Rees, the accompanist, D. J. Rees; treasurer, W. M. Williams and secretary, David Jones.

The Morriston Orpheus, National Winners Cup at Cardiff in 1960. The choir is pictured with accompanist Eufryn John, president Mr J. T. Morgan and Mrs Olwen Morgan alongside Revd Hubert Hughes and Ivor Sims.

The Morriston Orpheus Choir leaving for the Eisteddfod in Cardiff, 1960. Pictured outside the Parish Hall, Glantawe Street are, left to right: Stan Hope, -?-, Elaine Hope, Glyn Hopkins, Tom Elias, Greta Sims (wife of Ivor Sims), Peg David, -?-, Ivor Sims (founder and conductor), Ronnie Rees.

Above is a wonderful family photograph from 1902 of Elizabeth Jane Owen; her son, David John Owen and his daughter, Olga May Owen. Approximately ninety-three years later (around 1995) the photograph opposite completes five generations. Olga (photographed above) married Evan Jones. Their son David John Owen Jones is pictured opposite with his wife Marjorie and their children, Siân Ann and Paul Stuart. Their family home since 1902 has been Garden Terrace, off Morgan Street, later renamed Aran Street.

Ladies of Morriston Golf Glub attending a dinner at the Langland Bay Hotel in 1962.

Staff outing of Rees & Kirby, Morriston, c. 1950. The company was founded in 1898 and registered as a private company in 1900. The founders were Col. W. D. Rees, of Swansea, and Mr. S. C. Kirby, who came from the Lake District. Constructional steelwork built by this firm includes the Devil's Bridge near Aberystwyth in 1900. They were also responsible for the Slip Bridge built for the Swansea Corporation in 1914 over the Mumbles Road, Mumbles Railway and Victoria Line; all the steelwork for the Swansea Guildhall in 1931; the Cardiff Arms Park North double deck Grandstand in 1933 and the South Stand in 1955-56.

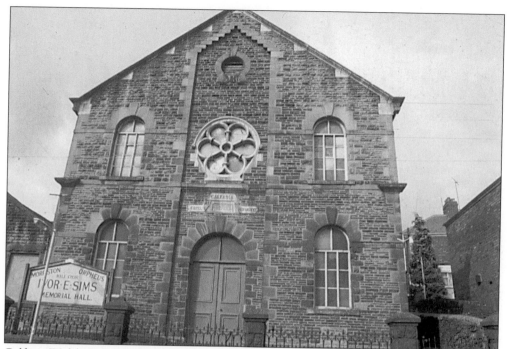

Calfaria Welsh Baptist chapel situated in Banwell Street in June 1986. The foundation stone was laid by Miss Mary Thomas of Market Street and in 1889 it opened its doors for worship for the first time. The chapel was demolished in 1991.

A play *Snow White and the Seven Dwarfs* held at Calfaria chapel in the 1940s.

Mr Ian Jones outside Sayers Discount shop (now Morriston Job Centre) during Morriston Shopping Fesival in 1978.

Below opposite: Carol singing outside St David's church in 1970. The vicar is again the Revd Hubert Hughes. The boys, left to right, front row: Simon Morris, Keith Thomas, Stuart Loosemoore, Andrew Hope, Nicholas Samuel, Mark Thomas.

St David's church Gibert & Sullivan Operatic Group in 1969. At the back in the centre is the Revd Hubert Hughes and the lady on the far left is the accompanist Lily Bowden Watts. The first Operatic Society came into being in the early 1920s and many were performed on the stage of the Bioscope Hall, known later as the Regal Cinema in Woodfield Street. In the 1960s, the vicar of St David's, the Revd Hubert Hughes, himself an excellent singer, revived the Opera Group. This society sang almost the entire work of Gilbert & Sullivan from the well known to the more obscure.

The bakery staff of Hunts, Bakers & Confectionery, in the 1950s. The Job Centre occupies the premises today. Note Tabernacle Tower in the background.

The Salvation Army (pictured here holding an open air service in 1958) has occupied these premises since May 1889. The hall in Morfydd Street was rededicated in 1992 after extensive refurbishment.

The Timbrel Section of the Salvation Army at Morriston, c. 1958. Left to right: Muriel Mead, Timbrel Leader, Gloria Mead, Pamela Davies, Janice Haeney, Joan Gower, Brenda Palmer, Margaret Harris, Brenda Williams, Dorothy Saunders, Gaynor Trotman, Susan Griffiths.

An old house at Morfydd Street in 1898. Standing on the door is Mary Walters and her son. The house was later demolished and on its site now is a 'Ted Morris' red brick row of houses, situated next door but one to the oldest house in Morriston.

Mr Sid Thonton, the proprietor of Wychtree Street's general store in 1954.

The members of Sunshine Corner outside Wychtree Street's Elim Meeting Hall in the early 1950s. 'Sunshine Corner all is jolly fine. Is for children under 99. All is welcome, seats are given free. Come to Sunshine Corner, that's the place for me.'

Shopkeepers and customers at Clase Road near Morriston Cross 1954. This is a wonderful example of a self-contained community within a community. The photograph shows, left to right Mrs William Hole, Mrs Theo Rogers, Mrs W. T. Rees, Mr and Mrs E. Robbins, Mr F. Rabbaiotti, Mrs E. Bruton.

The children of Margam Avenue in 1954. Pictured here, left to right, are: Christine Bradley, John Bradley, Barry Paine, Heather Daniels, Cynthia Weaver, George John Paine, Anthony Evans, Clive Jamas, Derek Miles.

Chatting at Glantawe Street bus depot forty-six years ago is driver Glan Jenkins, Billy Hole, Bryn Davies and Roy Thomas.

Ladies of Glantawe Street in June 1954. Left to right: Mrs K. Maddocks, Mrs M. L. Davies, Mrs L. Llewellyn, Mrs E. Francis, Anne Francis, Tegwyn Francis (just out of the photograph).

St John's church, in 1915. A church has stood on this site since 1789, but Swansea's most famous landmark is soon to disappear. Sadly, St John's has been neglected and although The Church of Wales has continued to maintain the building, insufficient funds mean that the time has come to end this, a very significant chapter in the history of Morriston.

SWANSEA

REGᴰ
TRADEMARK.

127

Acknowledgements

Having changed in my appearance (from the photograph on page 93) my passion for local history, however, still remains as strong as ever. Having collected old postcards, photographs and books on the locality since an early age and now after writing three successful books on Morriston, I decided at the age of twenty-seven years to write my first Swansea book. It was always my intention to include areas that have sometimes been ignored up until now and as a result I would sincerely like to thank everyone who has generously loaned photographs including Jim Watkins; Ivor Davies; Andrew Jones; Elaine & Stan Hope.

Without doubt, this book would not have been possible without the assistance received from Hywel Morris – a true friend – to whom I am very grateful too. Thank you to all my friends at Contractor Services department of Iechyd Morgannwg Health including Zoë Whetton; Carol Niven Wayne Casey and Martin Sullivan. Thank you to Rosemary Senra for here professional proof-reading, advice and emcouragement. Also thank you to my project editor, Jane Friel, for her patience with all those Welsh place names.

Throughout my thirteen years of writing books and at all other times my parents Joan and Denzil have supported and encouraged me. I would like to take this opportunity to thank them for always being there for me through music and local history.